Published by Scholastic Inc., *Publishers since 1920.*
SCHOLASTIC and associated logos are trademarks and/or
registered trademarks of Scholastic Inc. All rights reserved.

The publisher does not have any control over and does not assume
any responsibility for author or third-party websites or their content.

ISBN 978-1-338-26820-1

10 9 8 7 6 5 4 3 2 1   18 19 20 21 22
Printed in the U.S.A.   40

First printing 2018

Book design by Plum5 Limited
Written by Emily Ball

I Am JiFFPOM™

Scholastic Inc.

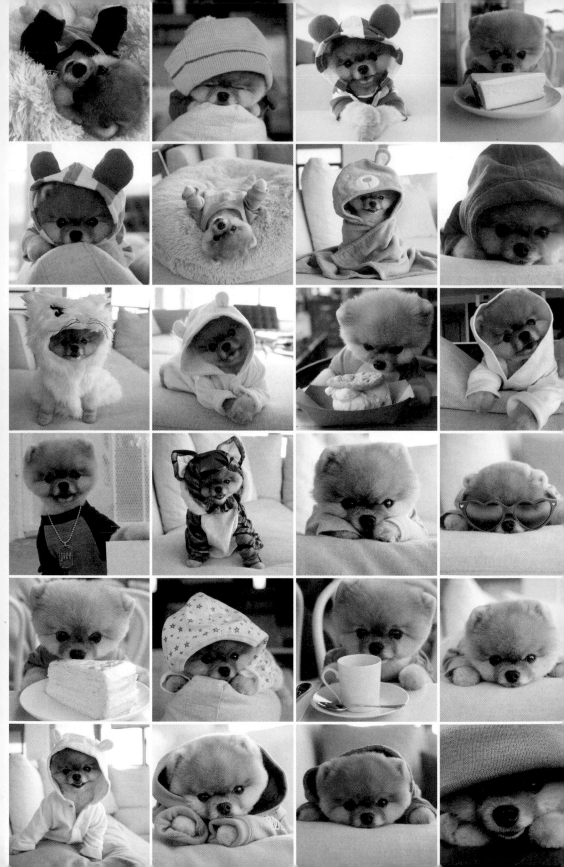

WHAT'S INSIDE?

MEET JIFFPOM!

Hi! I'm Jiffpom!

I'm a little pup with a big personality who loves having fun! From posing for photos to skateboarding, acting in music videos to winning Guinness World Records, I'm always busy and up for an adventure.

I do get some downtime though, when I like to sleep, eat, listen to music, and spend time with my friends. This is a book all about me — I hope you like it.

Love from,

Jiffpom™

♥

A DAY IN THE LIFE OF JIFFPOM

I'm a busy dog who likes to get out and about and see my friends. This is a day in my life.

First I wake up.

Why is it always so hard to get out
of bed in the morning?

I need to get ready!
I've got a big day ahead.

No matter what the weather throws
at me, I'm always prepared.

Brrr ... it's cold
out there.

This big hood
will keep me
dry in the rain.

Sunny skies mean sunglasses...

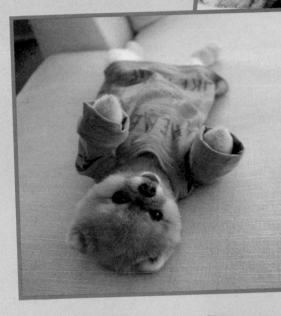

...and T-shirts!

All wrapped up and ready for snow.

Breakfast — the most important meal of the day.

Mmmm... I love the smell of fresh coffee in the morning.

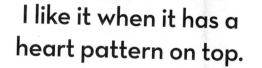

I like it when it has a heart pattern on top.

I can't wait to go out and have an adventure.

First, let's go shopping!

Can you carry me?

I love checking out all the great shops!

Do you like my new boots?

Sometimes I get stopped
to have my picture taken.

I try not to let the fame go to my head...

#CUTIE

...but I can't help being this cute.

Hooray — it's lunchtime.

Is this
for me?

This pizza
looks so
yummy.

Mmm . . .
smells good

Now it's time to see some friends. Who do you think I should meet up with today?

Here are some photos of me hanging out with my pals. Tick the box next to your favorite friend.

This is Tweetie

Snuffles makes me laugh

Meet Mr Reindeer

Now add a picture of yourself here so we can hang out today, too!

My paws
hurt from all
that fun.

Let's head
home!

I'm super sleepy. I might just close
my eyes for a second . . .

ZZZ

JIFFPOM
07

zZZ

Napping is great...

...but now it's time to chill out with a magazine and watch some TV.

I might also practice my skateboarding skills.

Look at me go!

Sometimes I go out to
fancy events and parties.

I always try to look my best.

Birthday parties are so much fun!

My present to you is me!

Dinnertime is my favorite part of the day.

Please don't make me share.

Look at this cupcake
— it's amazing.

 And so pink!

After a long day I like to have
a nice, warm bath.

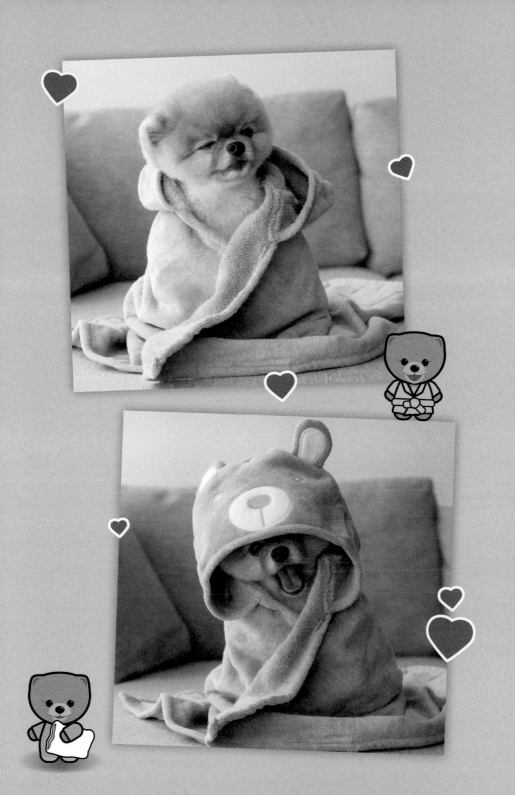

It's definitely time for bed now.

Yawn!
What a good day.

Sweet dreams, everyone.

I wonder what I'll
dream about tonight?

WHAT'S YOUR JIFFPOM PERSONALITY?

Want to discover which side of my personality suits you best? Answer the questions below to find out.

1. If you and I were to meet up, we would . . .

a. Get out of the house, meet new people, and do new things. Let's go on an adventure!

b. Watch a movie, play some computer games, take some selfies . . . anything relaxing.

c. Go skateboarding or running in the park! Being active and trying out new sports is always fun.

2. It's a rainy day and you're stuck inside, what do you do to pass the time?

a. Grab my boots and raincoat — there's plenty of fun to be had in the rain if you have the right attitude.

b. Snuggle up and put on a good movie. I love it when it rains — it gives me an excuse to stay inside and chill out.

c. Play a game with my friends or family. Just because I'm stuck inside doesn't mean I can't run around and be active.

3. It's Friday and you've got tons of homework to do. Do you . . .

a. Leave it in your bag until Monday morning. Weekends are for having fun!

b. Put it aside for now — I've got the rest of the weekend to think about it.

c. Do it right away, then I'll have the whole weekend to do exciting things.

4. Imagine yourself in ten years' time. Who do you see?

a. I'm a movie star on the red carpet, or a scientist who's cured a deadly disease. Whatever I end up doing, I'm going to make sure I'm remembered.

b. Ten years is so far away, I don't want to think about that yet. There's so much that can change. I'll just go with the flow and see what happens!

c. I'm a professional athlete representing my country in the Olympics. I want to be someone that puts all my energy to good use!

5. You decide to start up your own vlog. What's it about?

a. Traveling

b. Arts and crafts

c. Fitness and well-being

6. What's your favorite kind of music?

a. Anything and everything! There's no way I could decide on just one type of music. There's so much out there and not enough time to listen to it all.

b. My favorite kind of music is folk, acoustic, or chilled-out pop. I like relaxing to music, rather than dancing to it.

c. Pop music with a super-catchy beat is my favorite. Anything that gets me up and dancing!

YOU ARE . . .

Count up how many As, Bs, and Cs you scored on the questions from the previous pages to find out which side of my personality suits you the most.

MOSTLY As
Social Butterfly

You can't stand being cooped up and are always up for going out, seeing your friends, and being adventurous. Sometimes you find that your plans clash or you've been too busy and need a moment to chill, but not for too long. You want to get out and see and do as much as you can — just like me. You only live once!

MOSTLY Bs
Totally Chilled

I lead a busy life, but sometimes I just want to chill out with a good movie or book. That's just like you! Sure, it's great to get out and have fun, but you'd much rather have a nap in front of your favorite TV show and relax.

MOSTLY Cs
Active Achiever

You've got loads of energy and are always up for doing something that gets your heart racing — and I'm the same. From skateboarding to dancing, I'm always up for trying out a new activity, working hard, and doing my best.

JIFFPOM'S SELFIE SCHOOL

I always try to look my best in my photos. Do you want to learn how to be a selfie master like me? Follow my tips and you'll be a pro in no time.

Look straight into the camera.

A little head
tilt can go
a long way.

Or an extreme close-up.

Hi!

49

Don't worry.
Sometimes I get nervous, too.

For when you're feeling camera shy, try the "look-away" pose.

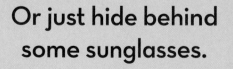

Or just hide behind some sunglasses.

Works every time.

Posing next to yummy food also seems to bring out my best features.

I didn't even realize this one was being taken!

Trying out different poses is important.

It helps to keep your look fresh.

Lying on my back is one
of my favorite positions.

Love

55

Keep your outfit choices varied.

Don't always wear the same thing.

Make a statement.

Here I am trying out a beard.

They'll never guess it's me!

The main thing is to smile, be confident, and be yourself.

Oh, and have fun!

The
perfect
shot!

#SELFIE

JIFFPOM'S FAVORITE THINGS

I might lead a busy life, but I still find time for hobbies. I love being active and getting out and about. These are just a few of the fun things I like doing.

I might be small but I've got tons of energy.

I love skateboarding . . .

love

LOVE

. . . and playing ball games.

Taking selfies is my best skill.

Did you know that I'm the most followed dog on Instagram?

#SELFIE

Dancing is also fun.

Let's dab!

#DAB

I love dressing up.
I've got a costume for every occasion!

Which outfit is your favorite? Pick which one you like the most.

Easter bunny Jiffpom

Hippy Jiffpom

Jiffpom in disguise

Santa Claus Jiffpom

My favorite time of year for costumes is Halloween. Don't I look scary?

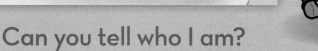

Can you tell who I am?

Does staring at cupcakes count as a hobby?

It's one of my favorites if it does.

And sleeping?

ZZz

69

ADORABLE ACTIVITIES

As well as being active, I like being creative and am always up for trying something new. Here are a few activities inspired by me for you to try.

Make Your Own Jiffpom Mask

Want to look as cute as me? Follow the simple steps below to create your very own Jiffpom mask. You can find the mask at the back of the book.

You will need:

· Scissors
· Glue stick
· Cardboard
· Hole punch
· 2 lengths of string or elastic (about 12 inches each)

TOP TIP:
Ask an adult to help you when using scissors!

How to make it:

1. Cut around the mask at the back of the book along the dotted lines. Stick it on to some cardboard.

2. Cut around the mask again, carefully cutting along the dotted lines around the eyes.

3. Using a hole punch, make two holes on either side of the mask where shown. Tie one piece of string or elastic through each hole.

4. Put your Jiffpom mask on and tie the string around your head to keep it in place.

5. Smile! You're looking pretty cute right now.

#CUTIE

Spot the Jifference

Can you spot the seven differences between the two pictures?
You'll find the answers at the back of the book.

CAPTURING CUTENESS

I'm only a little pup with a lot of growing up to do, but I've been told that I'm one of the most adorable dogs in the world! Here are just a few of my cutest moments. Which one do you like the most?

That time I was a tiger?

Watch out, I'm about to pounce.

Or a polar bear?

Grrrrrrr!

Who are you calling cute?

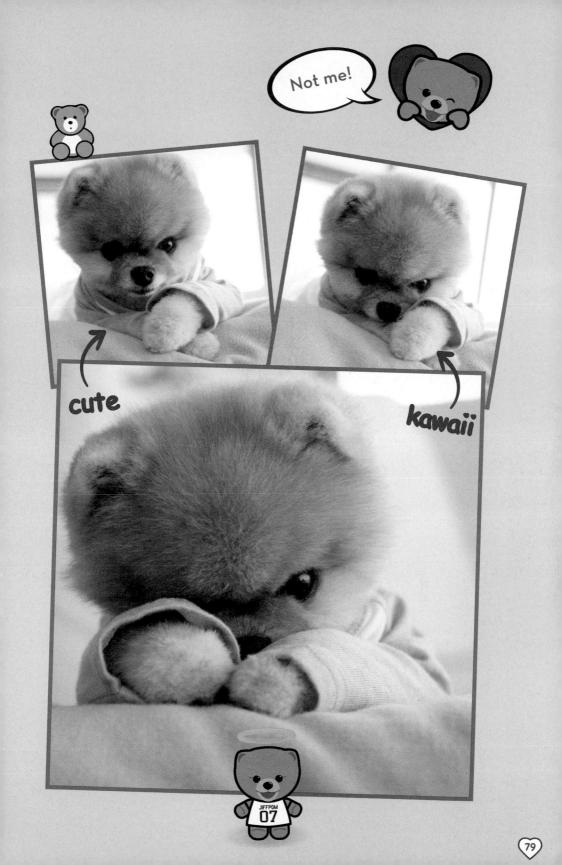

Not me!

cute

kawaii

JIFFPOM
07

79

I like hiding under big hats.

And wrapping up in cozy blankets!

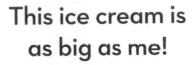

This ice cream is as big as me!

 What tasty treat is hiding
in that bowl?

Or bunny ears!

Cuteness is Real

ARE YOU A JIFFPOM GENIUS?

I might have over 20 million followers on social media, but how well do you actually know me? See if you can answer the eight questions below to find out!

1. How many Guinness World Records have I won?

a. 3

b. 5

c. 10

2. On which social media platform do I have the most followers?

a. Twitter

b. Musical.ly

c. Instagram

3. What's special about August 20th?

a. It's my birthday.

b. It's "JIFF Day" in LA.

c. It's my favorite day.

4. Where do I live?

a. On the moon

b. Hawaii

c. In LA

SMART

5. What's my favorite dance move?

a. I don't have one — I don't like dancing.

b. Dabbing

c. The moonwalk

6. Whose music video did I star in?

a. Katy Perry's

b. Justin Bieber's

c. Taylor Swift's

7. What kind of dog am I?

a. A Pomeranian

b. A Labrador

c. I'm not a dog, I'm a teddy bear.

8. What's my favorite sport?

a. Skateboarding

b. Soccer

c. Both of the above — I don't have a favorite!

Find the answers at the back of the book!

LOVE U

Thanks so much for
looking through my book — I hope
you had fun reading it. I'd like
to dedicate this book to all my fans.
Thank you for all your kind words and
great comments — this wouldn't have
been possible without you.

Lots of love,

Jiffpom.

Please also remember that I'm a very unique dog. Most
dogs wouldn't want you to put anything other than dog
food or a bone in their mouths and definitely wouldn't
let you dress them up in all kinds of outfits or teach them
how to skateboard. I guess that's what makes me special!

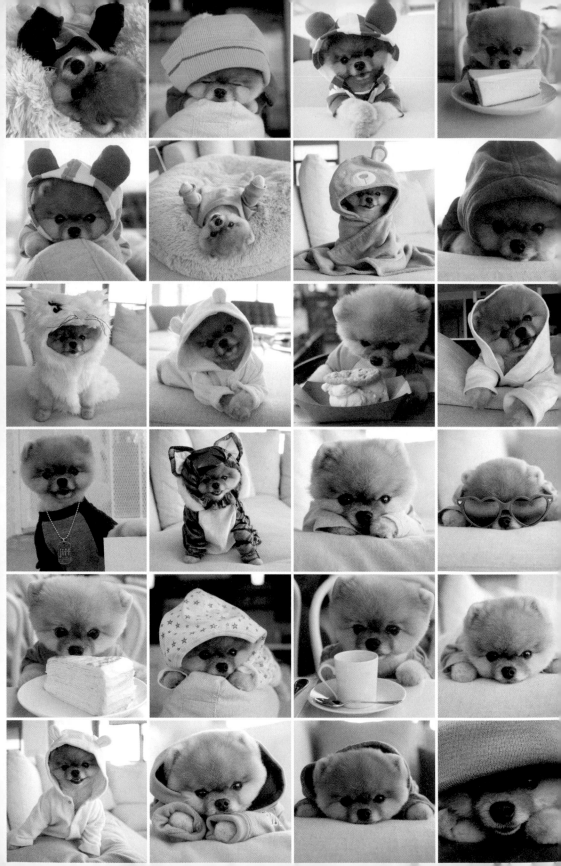

Page 72: Spot the Jifference

1) **Star behind bush**
2) **Piece of fence missing**
3) **Hat is now pink**
4) **Jiffpom is winking**
5) **His tongue is now orange**
6) **Jiffmoji in the bush**
7) **Present on the wall**

Pages 88-89: Are You a Jiffpom Genius?

1) a   2) b   3) b   4) c   5) b   6) a   7) a   8) c

MAKE YOUR OWN JIFFPOM MASK

Instructions on page 72

Ask an adult to help you when using scissors!

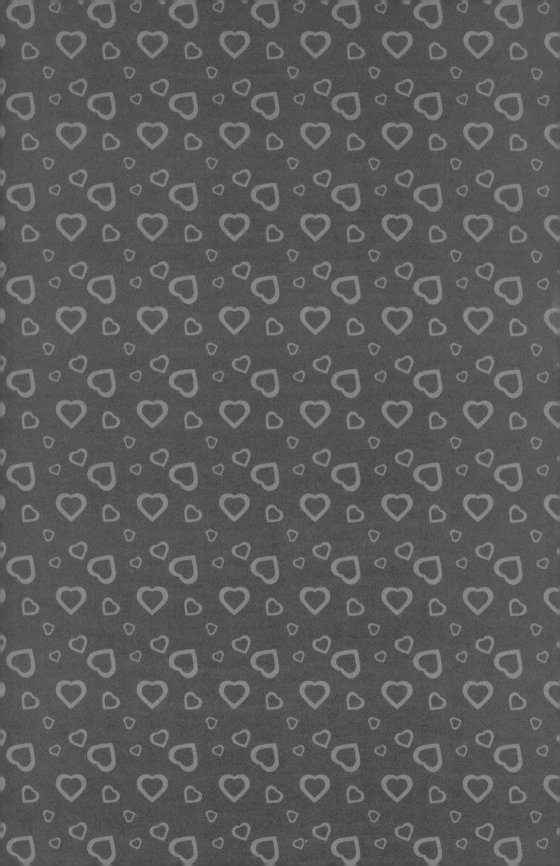